BUDDHIST WISDOM :
The Mystery of the Self

BUDDHIST WISDOM:
The Mystery of the Self

GEORGE GRIMM

Translated by
CARROLL AIKINS

Edited by
M. KELLER GRIMM

MOTILAL BANARSIDASS PUBLISHERS
PRIVATE LIMITED • DELHI

Reprint: Delhi, 1982, 1989, 1999, 2008
Second Revised Edition: Delhi, 1978

ISBN: 978-81-208-0510-1 (Cloth)
ISBN: 978-81-208-3291-6 (Paper)

MOTILAL BANARSIDASS
41 U.A. Bungalow Road, Jawahar Nagar, Delhi 110 007
8 Mahalaxmi Chamber, 22 Bhulabhai Desai Road, Mumbai 400 026
203 Royapettah High Road, Mylapore, Chennai 600 004
236, 9th Main III Block, Jayanagar, Bangalore 560 011
Sanas Plaza, 1302 Baji Rao Road, Pune 411 002
8 Camac Street, Kolkata 700 017
Ashok Rajpath, Patna 800 004
Chowk, Varanasi 221 001

PRINTED IN INDIA

BY JAINENDRA PRAKASH JAIN AT SHRI JAINENDRA PRESS,
A-45 NARAINA, PHASE-I, NEW DELHI 110 028
AND PUBLISHED BY NARENDRA PRAKASH JAIN FOR
MOTILAL BANARSIDASS PUBLISHERS PRIVATE LIMITED,
BUNGALOW ROAD, DELHI 110 007

PREFACE

This book by George Grimm has been translated from the German in the belief that it might awaken in the reader the desire to deepen his knowledge of the Teaching of Gotama the Buddha, and in particular, that it may serve as an introduction to George Grimm's standard-work *The Doctrine of the Buddha. The Religion of Reason and Meditation.* The Buddha himself describes his Teaching as "the clearly visible, at any time accessible, the all-inviting, which is called : 'Come and see', which is a guide and can be experienced by reasonable men in their own interior."

All thinking men realize that the ceaselessly changing physical body is not the true Self; and we are beginning to see what the Buddha saw over two thousand years ago: that the mental and so-called spiritual processes are, like the body, continually changing and can thus be described but as a succession of moments of consciousness. But what then is the true Self? What am I? Some people have come to the conclusion that there is no Self other than personality, which perishes with the body. The Buddha, however, shows us that there is no reason for such a conclusion and he definitely repudiates the accusation made against him, that he taught the annihilation of the true Self: "And I, monks, who speak thus and teach thus, am accused wrongly, vainly, falsely and inappropriately by some ascetics and Brahmins : 'A denier is the ascetic Gotama, he teaches the destruction, annihilation and perishing of the being that now exists.' These ascetics wrongly, vainly, falsely and inappropriately accuse me of being what I am not, and of saying what I do not say...Only one thing, monks, do I teach, now as before, namely suffering and the annihilation of suffering."

It is the purpose of this book to let the reader *see* that we actually do not consist in anything of the world. It shows us up that our true Self, the Tathāgata within us, is beyond space and time and therewith "immeasurable, unfathomable like the great Ocean."

C. Aikins

CONTENTS

Preface v

THE SELF

SECTION 1 The primitive Problem 1
2 The external world, as conveyed to me through the five outer senses, is not my Self 1
3 The mental objects (dhammā) are not my Self 1
4 My corporeal organism is not my Self 4
5 Cognition is not my Self 5
6 I am not a so-called soul 6
7 Willing is not my Self 7
8 The true Self 8

THE SUFFERING SELF

9 Will, the indefatigable "house-builder" 10
10 During my world-wandering I experience every possible sensation 10
11 Everything ends in suffering 11
12 The difficulty of recognizing any life as ending in suffering 12
13 Harm-producing sense-pleasures bring about the greatest suffering 13
14 Mean sense-pleasures lead to sorrowful rebirth 16
15 A survey of our world-wanderings 18
16 The heaven and hell-worlds in particular 19
17 The seeming impossibility of recollecting former existences 21

THE DELIVERED SELF

18 Our goal—the realization of the mind's deliverance 24
19 The relation between craving and the activity of the mind 27
20 The influence of the habitual tendencies on the organism 28

SECTION

21 The possibility of the deliverance of the mind 29
22 The annihilation of thirst through right cognition 32
23 In particular the desire to see or communicate with departed friends 33
24 The annihilation of craving for the own organism 35
25 The training of the thinking-faculty through its methodical development as prerequisite for right cognition 36
26 The gradual overcoming of thirst 39
27 The deliverance of the mind is the freedom in the use of our cognizing-apparatus 43
28 The bliss of non-willing 46

THE EXTINGUISHED SELF

29 The Self is transcendent : *all* concepts apply only to the Not-Self (anattā) 50
30 The concept of extinction in particular 51
31 The concept of nothingness 55
32 The Absolute State 57
33 The "submerging in one's own depths"; the immeasurability of the Absoute State 57
34 The realm of Essences 60
APPENDIX 62

THE SELF

§ 1

THE PRIMITIVE PROBLEM

The primitive problem is not : "What is the *world*?" but : "What am *I* ?" For it is certainly possible that in case I know what *I* am, the world does not interest me any more.

§ 2

THE EXTERNAL WORLD, AS CONVEYED TO ME THROUGH THE FIVE OUTER SENSES, IS NOT MY SELF

The forms I see with the eyes, the sounds I hear with the ears, the scents I smell with the nose, the flavours I taste with the tongue, the objects I touch with my body as organ of touch, have nothing to do with *me*, with my true Self. If these various objects of my organs of sense would vanish, I myself should nevertheless still be; their destruction would not touch my true Self. Thus it is quite evident that the external world, as conveyed to me through the five organs of sense, has nothing to do with my true Self.

§ 3

THE MENTAL OBJECTS (DHAMMĀ) ARE NOT MY SELF

We have not only five but six senses. The sixth sense-activity is *thinking*, effected with the organ of thought. The objects of this sense of thinking are all objects of the five outer senses and their causal relations to one another, i.e. all possible *phenomena* of the external world. Of these phenomena I construct, by means of the organ of thought, the pictures of imagination and the abstract concepts or ideas. They are the specific objects of the organ of thought; as mere *products* of the latter (which I may or may not allow to arise) they naturally have nothing to do with my true Self.

But the organ of thought has a further object : infinite space. We recognize space by mere thinking, and therefore also when the activity of the five outer senses is wholly at rest. Space is the *immediate* object of the sense of thought : in the very moment we begin to think, space becomes evident. Now any activity of the five outer senses immediately entails the activation of the organ of thought; this is the reason for our perceiving space at the very moment of any sense-activity. Thus we cannot recognize any external object without recognizing at the same time the space in which it is. On the other hand, we can cognize space alone, namely by bringing the activity of the five outer senses to a complete standstill and by concentrating the organ of thought solely upon space (mental perception of infinite space).

We may as well eliminate space itself from our thinking and *yet* think, namely thus : we wholly appease the activity of the outer senses and direct the organ of thought, in absolute concentration, upon the thought : "there no longer exists anything for me". Thus even space is eliminated from *con-*

sciousness and only the thought "there no longer exists anything" is left over.

But not only can we eliminate space from our consciousness but we can realize directly that space has *objectively* nothing whatever to do with with our true Self: Let us imagine the impossible, that all space outside my body were to be annihilated. This very fact would not touch *me* at all. There remains the question whether the space occupying my body is essential to me. Let us now imagine this body, with unimpaired vitality, shrunk to the size of Tom Thumb : I would *intuitively* recognize that the space which *had* occupied my body formerly, when it was taller, has nothing at all to do with my essence. It is obvious that I myself should not have become *less* by this diminution of my body (what ought to have happened if the space occupying my body were essential to me); on the contrary, despite my body now being smaller and the space occupying it lesser, I should still recognize myself as the same I have always been.

In the same way, the space on the moon doesn't concern me either. It might as well disappear, I know that I shall in no way be touched thereby. Therefore, even the space in which I live in this very moment doesn't concern me. The state of affairs is as follows : even space is not my true Self, because I perceive its arising and passing away *for me*.

Thus it is evident, that even space cannot have anything to do with *me*, with my true Self; it is merely the condition for the existence of my *body*.

§ 4

MY CORPOREAL ORGANISM IS NOT MY SELF

The question now is, which is my relation to my *body*. The latter consists entirely of materials of the *external world*, which I grasp in the form of nourishment and which I *assimilate*, i.e. transform into the chemical compounds of which the matter of my body consists. This assimilation takes place in the following way: constantly used-up materials are being eliminated and new ones absorbed (metabolism). Thus, my body is *manifestly* non-essential to me : a short time ago the materials building it up were components of the external nature, from which I first had to *draw* them.

Let us imagine that the materials building up our body wouldn't need being assimilated (transformed), i.e. that they were all present in the body in their original condition. Thus we could *directly* and *intuitively* recognize our whole body with all its organs to be a mere assemblage of grasped materials of the external nature, incessantly flowing in and out; we ourselves *watch* this inflow and outflow, at the same time *regulating* it. In particular we should directly recognize blood as being mere water, in which the foodstuffs broken up and dissolved by digestive and glandular action are carried about; moreover, we should observe in direct intuition how the various tissues of the body are supplied with the necessary materials by the bloodstream, which at the same time carries the used-up materials towards the excretive organs. (App. a.)

Thus I do not consist in my corporeal organism but I merely *have* it.

§ 5

COGNITION IS NOT MY SELF

I effect the so-called mental functions with the sense-organs of my organism (which of course too consist of the materials of the external world), i.e. I see forms with the eyes, hear sounds with the ears, smell scents with the nose, taste flavours with the tongue, touch objects with the body and think mental objects with the organ of thought. It is obvious that, if I did not possess any sense-organs, I could neither see nor hear, nor smell, taste or touch; in particular, I could not think without an organ of thought. Thus these mental functions are *bound to the sense-organs and conditioned by them.*

Now to see, hear, smell, taste, touch and think is simply = to sense and to perceive : If I see a form with the eyes, visual sensation and visual perception arise; if I hear a sound with the ear, auditive sensation and auditive perception arise, and so on.

Now to sense and to perceive is to become conscious of something or to cognize.

Thus we have found that also seeing, hearing, smelling, tasting, touching and thinking, hence any sensation and perception and therewith any becoming conscious or cognizing have nothing to do with our true Self : all these processes are *brought about* by the evidently non-essential corporeal organism and thus are *conditioned* by it. Now if the organ, with which I produce something, is non-essential to me, naturally its product is all the more: "How could the mind be the Self, since it is brought about by what is not the Self?" (anattasambhūto mano kuto attā bhavissati ?).

§ 6

I AM NOT A SO-CALLED SOUL

According to the preceding enquiry, our corporeal organism is the *apparatus* by which we see, hear, smell, taste, touch and think (i.e. cognize) the objects of the external world; in short, it is our cognizing-apparatus. It is merely through this *apparatus* that we can come into contact with the world; at its breaking up all sensations and perceptions of the world will be done with.

Moreover, we may recognize even this cognizing-apparatus, by means of itself, in all its parts when we use it with this purpose; in other words: we can judge and master cognition through our cognizing-activity.

As we cannot cognize but by means of our cognizing-apparatus, which is not essential to us, our true Self does not consist in a soul either, for we suppose a soul to be an entity *consisting* in cognition, the latter not being a mere function of the cognizing-apparatus but of my own; thus it ought to be able, if necessary, to cognize just as well without sense-organs and consequently without a corporeal organism.

Such a soul cannot exist, for it is absurd to declare that there could be any sensation and perception, i.e. cognition, without sense-organs : to assume a cognition independent from cognizing-organs is like assuming a digestion without organs of digestion.

Strictly speaking, to say "*I* see, *I* hear, *I* think" is as erroneous as for a machinist to say "*I* discharge steam". Just as the machinist only causes the steam-engine to discharge steam, I merely cause the *will* to make use of my cognizing-apparatus to arise; with this *cognizing-apparatus* I then bring forth sensations, perceptions and in particular thoughts.

In this denial of the existence of a cognizing soul or spiritual entity supposed to exist independently from the corporeal organism, the Buddha drew a distinguishing line between himself and other religious teachers.

§ 7

WILLING IS NOT MY SELF

It is by desire or *will* that I am connected with my cognizing-apparatus : I *want* an organism and I *want* to make use of it. This will I try to satisfy through the six sense-organs whenever it aims at the generation of cognition, and in so far as the will aims at the vegetative functions, i.e. the functions meant to preserve my organism, through the organs concerned with those functions (heart, lungs, liver, etc.).

But even this will is not essentially connected with my true Self. On the contrary, it arises only under a specific condition, namely that of a cognized object appearing desirable, i.e. worthy of being wanted. In the very moment I realize that the sight of a certain object is but painful, the will to see it vanishes; and were I to recognize that *whatever* objects may enter my consciousness by the eyes bring about *only* a sorrowful sight, *any* willing would necessarily vanish, i.e. I should be without any will to see whatsoever. The same conclusions apply to the will I endeavour to satisfy through the other sense-organs, including the organ of thought. Thus I *am not* the will but I merely *have* a will; for this reason I may just as well have it *not*, without being thereby touched in my essence. Accordingly, the will is not my Self either.

§ 8

MY TRUE SELF

If I do subtract all those components which I have recognized as not being essentially mine from my Self — i.e. the will (wi), the corporeal organism (o) as well as the cognizing-activity (c) based on it and the world (wo) which comes into appearance for me through the cognizing-activity,— my true Self results in:

SELF — (wi+o+c+wo).

The Buddha calls the non-essential components of me enclosed in brackets "attributes" (upādhis) : I merely *assumed* them ; in reality they do not appertain to me.

If I now consider those attributes more closely, I realize that they comprehend all what is cognizable. Let us put it to proof: What remains for cognition when not only the whole external world has ceased to exist, but also any cognizing-activity, as well as my corporeal organism and even any willing ? Literally nothing. In fact, "everything" ceases. That this "everything" is but everything *cognizable*, and consequently, that the remaining "nothing" is only nothing *cognizable*, becomes clear by the fact that my true Self has in no way been touched by all these subtractions, inasmuch as we have recognized all what we have taken away from it as *not*-self. Thus my true Self lies beyond all cognition and hence beyond the world as the sum of everything cognizable. It is the Unknowable, the Unfathomable; it is *nec taliter, nec aliter, sed totaliter aliter*: it is neither so nor different but totally different.

§ 9

WILL, THE INDEFATIGABLE "HOUSE-BUILDER"

It is necessary clearly to realize, i.e. to *see* that the corporeal organism is something entirely different from me. If I *really* comprehend this, I shall as a consequence realize that the beginning and the end of this organism are not the beginning and the end of *myself*, but merely of this very organism. The question arises, how it comes that I possess the latter. The answer is rather simple: I am in connection with my organism merely through my *will*. It is only this will which procures me an organism, and it does so in the same and only way in which I procure whatever I want to possess, namely by *grasping* it: because I have the will for a corporeal organism I *grasp* the germ prepared by my parents, I *cling* to it for building up a corporeal organism. This process I repeat from time immemorial and I shall, if necessary, repeat perpetually; that is, as long as I have a *will* for a new organism when at the moment of *death* my actual body is snatched away from me.

§ 10

DURING MY WORLD-WANDERINGS I EXPERIENCE EVERY POSSIBLE SENSATION

Accordingly, it is not I who is constantly changing

but the corporeal organism as the immediate object of my willing, and, of course, the objects sensed and perceived through it. I myself am but unceasingly *impressed* by the sensations called forth by my organism. This applies not only to the brief interval between birth and death in the present life, but to the whole chain of my rebirths circling through countless billions of aeons : the whole scale of pleasant sensations, all conceivable indifferent sensations and above all the multitude of painful ones, as are those due to sickness or to any other misfortune. In particular I have experienced, innumerable times in the course of the world-aeons and in ceaseless succession, the sensation of dying; and since all possibilities must exhaust in the course of endless time, I have endured and suffered all possible deaths : death of tormenting sickness, on the battlefield. as a condemned murderer on the scaffold and so on.

§ 11

EVERYTHING ENDS IN SUFFERING

Thus I do swim in an immense sea of impermanence: whatever I experience continually changes to something else. There is no sensation of joy which does not pass, no sensation of sorrow which does not recur with inevitable certainty. Every pleasure is shadowed (even while being enjoyed) by the prospect that it too will pass with the passing of the object which caused it, only to be replaced by suffering; this will be the greater, the greater the joy was. The greatest suffering, however, we experience at the hour in which our own corporeal organism and hence the whole actual world is snatched away from us. We are then overwhelmed with sorrow, only to re-appear in a new form, exposed to new life, to new sickness, new decrepitude and death, and so forth in endless repetition. Who, having grasped the whole circle, would not be filled with horror and fright?

§ 12

THE DIFFICULTY OF RECOGNIZING ANY LIFE AS ENDING IN SUFFERING

Certainly the wise man too perceives, in this sea of impermanence which sweeps away *everything*, several aspects of happiness: the laughter of childhood, the joy of youthful lovers, the pleasure of bodily lust, a mother's delight in her child; he knows and hears the exultations, the cries of delight of all those whose wishes have been fulfilled. But above all and beyond all this he knows and hears the grief and the wailing of parents at the death of their children, the suffering of the sick and needy, the despair of the poor and friendless, the anguish of the dying.

Naturally, only the *wise* hears like this. The average man *is not willed* to hear such cries of sorrow; he removes from his sight and hearing everything that might thwart his craving for pleasant sensations. Thus he puts the poor in poorhouses, the sick in hospitals, the insane in asylums, the criminals in prison, so that he may enjoy undisturbed the illusion of a pleasurable world. He even does romanticize death, stifling with flowers the unpleasant odours of putrefaction. But does he *lessen* misery by trying to cover it over? Does he reduce suffering by simply ignoring it?

It is rather difficult to make a true valuation of life. Our feeble, undeveloped cognizing-faculty, which normally is scarcely more efficient than that of the higher animals, is able to apprehend only a very brief period of time, namely the immediate present we live in. Taking into account this common defect in cognition, let us now try to imagine a period of eighty years with all its experiences reduced to a span of less than one hour. We should see, within a few minutes, the infant become a child, the child a youth, the youth a young man, a lover; we should see the lover embrace his wife, who, like himself, grows older in this very moment, losing grace, charm, beauty, vigour, thus becoming, as the seconds go by, feeble, haggard, bent, wrinkled, toothless and decrepit; finally, just while the man is trying to make out what it is all about, we should observe him being befallen by old-age and decrepitude. This perfectly true picture of life, summed up in quick-motion, shows clearly enough the worthlessness of all events and hence of life on the whole. Is it not a rather horrifying prospect to consider that all this might recur endlessly?

§ 13

HARM-PRODUCING SENSE-PLEASURES BRING ABOUT THE GREATEST SUFFERING

The only thing that seems to us worthy of being desired is pleasant sensation; we do not take any interest in the neutral ones, and the painful ones we directly shun.

With regard to the pleasant sensations called forth by sense-pleasures, the Buddha declares, that in so far as they do not cause any harm to other beings and as they are aimed at nobler states of mind, they are not to be avoided by the average man. What is more, he declares certain noble sense-pleasures to be essential components of the Noble Path: friendliness and sympathetic joy towards the other beings, two of the four "Immeasurables", also called the four *Holy States* (brahmavihārā). (Cf. § 26)

On the other hand, mean, harm-producing sense-pleasures entail the greatest suffering. This the average man doesn't understand. Yet the complete agreement of the saints of all religions and times on this subject, should make him ponder over this fact. All those morally excelling men were filled with the deepest love for the fellow-beings, thus seeking not only their own happiness but that of the latter too. This their desire for well-being certainly would have made them indulge in mean sense-pleasures and recommend others to do likewise, had they not discovered that they inevitably lead to sorrow. The Buddha declares: "If, monks, the overcoming of evil would result in harm and in sorrow, I should not say that ye must overcome evil". Thus the condemnation of harm-producing sense-pleasures has the clearest foundation in the teaching of the Buddha:

Craving (tanhā, thirst) for sense-pleasures reigns in us, dominates us, and we seek its satisfaction or calming by activating our sense-organs since their non-satisfaction entails but grief and suffering. "Not to obtain what one longs for — that is suffering". But we shun suffering like the plague. Now all desire within us is only aimed at sense-pleasures; therefore our whole activity is aimed at attaining as many sense-pleasures as possible to avoid suffering. However, desire has one unfortunate characteristic: it cannot be *definitively* satisfied by any sense-pleasure, since they are all *impermanent.* Thus desire is literally insatiable. Consequently we are led by it on a never-ending pursuit of pleasure, an eternal will-o'-the-wisp, and it grows stronger with each momentary satisfaction, finally assuming a quite terrifying power. Moreover, every worldly pleasure turns to suffering on the passing of the object which had caused it; it does so in exact proportion: the greater the joy, the greater the suffering. "Food and drink turn to faeces and urine — pleasure turns to suffering", declares the Buddha. This quality of worldly sense-pleasures being ultimately unsatisfying is what first makes them displeasing to the clear-seeing man.

The second and far more serious aspect of worldly sense-pleasures is the following: any suffering arises from impeded willing. Consequently, any suffering ceases with the giving-up of any craving. Being desireless, boundless peace descends upon us, which states that craving no longer disturbs us. He who is free from desire is also free from the anxiety and suffering it entails. In fact, he who succeeds in giving up all craving is as happy as he who might succeed in obtaining *all* worldly honours, luxuries and so on. Both would possess *everything* they desire, the will of both of them would be appeased; and appeased will is happiness. There is but one fundamental difference: utmost richness can only be achieved temporarily, while utmost desirelessness we can realize at any time and for ever.

This highest degree of desirelessness and therewith highest bliss has been experienced by the saints, as the annihilation of the "enticing and poisonous craving". For that very reason they disdain and despise the deceptive, momentary sense-pleasures, finding them "mean and filthy", all the more as they do cause craving to increase thus separating us more and more from the *true* happiness of freedom from will. Therefore they warn us against worldly sense-pleasures as the greatest obstacle in our quest for happiness.

This makes clear how erroneous it would be to take as guide on this quest for happiness (a thing other than happiness nobody seeks) men, who do know only the happiness of worldly sense-pleasures. Only the saints can make real and safe guides, for they know by own experience the *bliss* beyond the worldly pleasures of senses, and thus may lead us towards its pure atmosphere.

§ 14

MEAN SENSE-PLEASURES LEAD TO SORROWFUL REBIRTH

I am, in myself, nothing of this world. In particular I am not a man either; I have merely grasped the sort of "attributes" (upādhis) which presently *make* me a human one. As I am nothing of the world and am thus not *determined* by anything, I may, on the death of my body, grasp whatever possible germ, be it in a woman's womb or in an animal's, in a world of light or in the lower worlds we call hell; thus I either become a human being again or an animal, a heavenly being or a hellish one. Such prospects frighten the modern man, what only proovse his lack of courage for thinking to its end a doubtlessly correct thought: of course I could never become an animal if I were essentially a human being. But what I am now, namely a man, I am *not* essentially; I merely "assumed" my actual organism which makes me a man. For this very reason, I may become an animal just as well as a man. And I can assume any other organism and I shall do so if I have the craving for doing so. At the moment of my death, when I am compelled to relinquish my actual organism as my *cognizing-apparatus*, I shall be wholly blind; thus I grasp a new germ, which is in harmony with my innermost *craving*, a germ having *affinity* to it, no matter whether it be a human germ, an animal one or a germ of any other world. Later, when this germ has developed to an organism, I shall recognize myself, in the light of the consciousness it produces, as a man, as an animal, a god or a devil. It is, thus, the quality of my actual *craving* which determines the nature of my future rebirth: the more brutal the sense-pleasures I now long for, the lower the realms to which I shall cling at the moment of death; conversely, my coming residence necessarily will be a world of light if I now feel a craving for *noble* sense-pleasures. This sensual differentiation according to the quality of desire or craving, is clearly noticeable between man and animal, and even more between man and man: we cannot conceive a highly moral man as grossly sensual, least of all as lascivious (lasciviousness being the focus of gross sensual passion), while we classify a man who indulges unrestrainedly and brutally in the satisfaction of harmful desires as a delinquent. Now at the moment of death each being clings to the very realm which is most in harmony with its craving: the moral man in a pure world, in a world of light, the beastly man in the world of beasts and the diabolic one in the world of devils. How could it be otherwise? He who denies this, also denies the law of affinity in chemistry, which, as any real law, is merely the specific application of a universal law. (App. b.)

§ 15

A SURVEY OF OUR WORLD-WANDERINGS

We now got a general survey of our sojourn in the world: from time immemorial we are wandering within its various realms, now clad in a human organism, now in an animal one, in heavenly or in hellish form. Thus, through the very organism we have "assumed", sensations continually arise within us, painful ones and joyful ones, in unceasing change, whereat the joyful sensations ultimately change over to sorrowful ones, thus themselves turning to sensations worthy of being hated. Who wants to taste a savoury drink knowing that it is poisoned and that he shall have to endure the painful consequences, although it be only many years afterwards? This simile often made use of by the Buddha cannot be pondered deeply enough, for thus being contemplated, even the joys of the highest worlds lose any attraction: even the sojourn in those heavenly worlds is, as everything in the world, *impermanent.* Accordingly and with regard to the endlessness of the circle of rebirths, in which all possibilities must exhaust, we shall with time inevitably again plunge into "wholly sorrowful" abodes, where the former heavenly joys will be forgotten and where suffering will keep its grasp on us again. Thus our whole world-wandering may be exhaustively characterized with the following words: "Only suffering arises where something arises; only suffering ceases where something ceases".

§ 16

THE HEAVEN AND HELL-WORLDS IN PARTICULAR

The preceding elucidation about ourselves and our relationship to the world might appear to be rather shocking. Nevertheless, it is of absolute solidity. For this reason, our very insight too will become as solid itself, if only we focus it prolongedly and thoroughly enough on the problem. We then recognize directly that it is so and cannot be otherwise, despite the ocean of suffering in which we thereby find ourselves submerged.

One point, however, seems not to be accessible to immediate cognition: the existence of hells and of heavenly worlds into which we likewise may be reborn. This circumstance weighs so heavily with certain people, that they reject the whole teaching of the Buddha because of it. To do so is, of course, as foolish as generally repudiating an epoch-making scientific work, filled with irrefutable information, just because one is unable to follow its statements on a specific subject. The understanding man, however, admired at the author's keen insight for the rest, will be rather inclined also to accept the statements he does not clearly understand, blaming himself for the problem being beyond his grasp. Wouldn't it be the height of folly to reject all the evident truths because of this one point? In the same way, he who despite the Buddha's excelling wisdom for the rest, doesn't rely on his statement that he knows those realms unaccessible to normal intuition by own experience, may just reject the subject he doesn't grasp: in all its other parts, the Buddha's doctrine will in no way thereby be touched, for *these* parts are accessible to immediate insight.

The existence of those realms can, however, be ascertained by him who has no immediate insight into them, with the same certainty with which the astronomer Le Verrier confirmed the existence of the planet Neptune by mere calculation: the supposition that the inexhaustible nature was capable of bringing about only forms of existence accessible to *our* sense-organs in the limitless universe (and not also such ones being organized differently, far higher and more subtle than the organisms *we* know), is to be regarded as absolutely out of the question. Those other beings are not separated from us by spatial barriers but by a difference in the threshold of consciousness. Thus the heavenly beings, the gods, are not "in the intervals of world" as Epicurus said, but "in the intervals of our perception of world". Anyway, such considerations may make objectively plausible the existence of those worlds, which so many saints, and in particular the Buddha, declare to have experienced by own intuition. For this reason there is no reasonable motivation for refusing the statements of those holy men incapable of any intentional lie, statements which are in perfect accordance despite thousands of years and miles separating them. This confidence in their unobjectivable testimonies too is a method for achieving the cognition of truth, and it is the most frequently applied one in everyday life.

§ 17

THE SEEMING IMPOSSIBILITY OF RECOLLECTING FORMER EXISTENCES

The fact that we cannot recollect our former existences is no *objection* to the doctrine of reincarnation: we do not remember so many events of our early childhood either and yet we have doubtlessly lived it. It is, at most, an uncleared part of the doctrine. But not even this is correct : recollection *is* possible, provided that the corresponding *faculty* has been developed, just as any other faculty must be first developed. I myself do not speak Chinese, and the gentle reader most probably doesn't either. Does this proove that nobody speaks Chinese? One hundred years ago travelling by air was regarded as impossible; nowadays it is an everyday event. Why could it be held to be impossible for so long? Because the prerequisites, the conditions of flying were unknown; consequently there was no development of the art of flying and therewith no training either. In the same way, we everyday persons do not know the prerequisites for the recollection of our former existences and therefore we cannot develop the corresponding faculty. Now does that mean that it is altogether impossible and that it shall be so for ever ? As a matter of fact, the Buddha and his noble disciples declare that they were capable of recollecting their former existences. What is more, the Buddha exactly informs us on the conditions required, so that it depends entirely on our realizing them. How narrow-minded must one be to speak of the impossibility of remembering former existences in the present state of affairs. At most one has the right to speak of one's own lack of energy, which makes us incapable of fulfilling those prerequisites. (App. c.) However, so it is usually, in particular also with regard to the great discoveries of natural science: almost every discovery has been declared to be impossible, even after having already been confirmed. Consequently, those who have confirmed it are sure to become an object of general derision whenever their discovery is too much at variance with the prevailing views. Thus one of the most ingenious physicists, J. R. Mayer, the discoverer of the principle of the conservation of energy, has been driven mad by the attacks and innuendoes on the part of the scientists. An everyday brain, capable of grasping but everyday events, doesn't become wider by dealing with sciences. Even the scientist himself only too often cannot distinguish the bounds of his own cognizing-faculty from those of absolute cognition. Thus he is always ready to protest against the doctrine of the Buddha : his understanding is not qualified for grasping it.

Moreover, it is an essential requisite for the further existence of the world, that the beings do *not* recollect their former existences. In case they would, they necessarily would at the same time see intuitively all the suffering they underwent for millions of years, in particular the suffering of ever recurring death. Thus they would either despair or in the same moment annihilate any craving for life, so that they would not be reborn any more; therewith the world would die out.

THE DELIVERED SELF

§ 18

OUR GOAL — THE REALIZATION OF THE MIND'S DELIVERANCE

I myself am beyond the phenomenal world. I am connected with it through my corporeal organism. I make use of its different organs, particularly of its cognizing-organ, to see, hear, smell, taste, touch and think (i.e. to sense and to perceive) the world as it manifests itself. For this reason my corporeal organism has the quality of being an *apparatus* for cognizing the world, that is, a *cognizing-apparatus.*

If the preceding elucidations would exhaustively explain how matters stand, (i.e. if there really were nothing but I myself, my corporeal organism whose organs I activate and the world as object of my cognizing-activity), the situation in which I am would be clear : I could decide at any time whether I should make further use of my cognizing-apparatus or throw it away. Now in reality, as we know, we are not free in our decision. We are constantly influenced by an alien factor, to such a degree, that even great geniuses declare the deliverance from this influence not to be achievable, while the Christian Churches, though they admit the possibility of liberation, declare it to be realizable only through the mercy of an almighty God.

Now what kind of influence hinders us in our free decision, sometimes to the degree of absolute dependence ? We do know it already: it is the *craving* (tanhā) within us. Whenever we try to make resistance to it, we *suffer* — suffering is impeded craving — to such a degree, that normally nobody takes courage for opposing it. For this very reason craving is generally held to be unconquerable. What we use to call craving, we also call will, greed, wish, desire, longing. All these and similar expressions serve to express one and the same fundamental phenomenon: to say "I want something", or "I crave for something", or "I wish, I desire, I long for something" comes to the same thing. Yet in particular the word *craving* (the Buddha says *thirst*) expresses the very nature of willing with utmost clearness: on closer examination of ourselves, we recognize any will as a sinitser (and therewith non-essential) might arising within us, and which violently *compels* us to make use of our organism (as the apparatus for satisfying this craving) in a quite specific manner.

Accordingly, the problem of deliverance is absolutely clear. It may be elucidated as follows : Can we free ourselves from the craving for making use of our cognizing-apparatus in a specific direction, or can we not ? If we can, that is, if we achieve wholly to deliver ourselves from craving or will, we shall be absolutely free in the use of our six-senses-apparatus : What inner hindrances ever could restrict him in this use, who is no longer influenced by any craving or will ? In all his activities he may decide in accordance with his actual cognition, without any inner opposition. If he recognizes something to be worth-while he sets to its realization, if not, he just doesn't take any trouble. Whatever he should be bent on he relinquishes without any grief at the very moment he recognizes it not to be achievable, for he is not compelled by craving further to strive for it. Furthermore, he gives up any project which in the course of its execution prooves unworthy or too strenuous, without feeling in the slightest degree ill-humoured at his activity being impeded. Whatever he does, he does with undisturbed calmess, with perfect equanimity and therewith with absolute peace of mind. Thus constantly he is absolutely happy. Could there be any felicity higher than boundless, unshakeable inner peace ?

The Buddha calls this condition the state of *deliverance of the mind* (cetovimutti). By mind is to be understood the sum of all mental functions, i.e. the activity of the six senses, including intuitive and logical thought. In these functions, that is in the use of the six-senses-apparatus (cognizing-apparatus), he who is delivered from any *influence* (āsava) by whatever craving or will is wholly *free*. Thus the problem of freedom from will in the doctrine of the Buddha properly is the problem of the *deliverance of the mind.*

According to the preceding statements, the deliverance of the mind at the same time is identical with true happiness. Now the Buddha teaches precisely the path to absolute deliverance of mind and therewith to *true* happiness. This happiness he calls the felicity of *holiness*. Thus we see that the concept of holiness, nowadays rather vague and incomprehensible, has a definite meaning in the Buddha's doctrine : it just means the achievement of absolute deliverance of the mind. Considering holiness from *this* point of view, is there anybody who would not desire to become holy ?

§ 19

THE RELATION OF CRAVING TO THE ACTIVITY OF THE MIND

Before taking up the question of the possibility of a deliverance from craving, it seems advisable first to state the way in which craving acts on the activity of our mind.

Craving manifests itself in three forms : as greed, as hatred and as delusion. Greed and hatred concern the sense-objects, while the delusion refers to the influence which craving has fundamentally and in particular on our cognizing-activity : we are, as we know, constantly compelled to think in a wrong manner, namely as though in spite of all we would consist in the components of our personality (see § 2 to 7), as if we should belong to the world and ought to occupy ourselves with its affairs for being happy.

As soon as our cognizing-activity is being influenced by one of those three fundamental manifestations of craving, and according to the quality of that influence, there arise in *us* the different *habitual tendencies* (sankhārā), such as joy, sadness, rage, hate, fear, love and so on. If we should manage to confront our cognizing-activity independently with the craving surging up within us (i. e. if we should manage to regard craving as an enemy who tries to force our cognizing-activity in a specific direction while we want it to be wholly unbiased), no habitual tendencies would ever arise. Thus the habitual tendencies are the product of craving having an influence on our cognizing-activity.

§ 20

THE INFLUENCE OF THE HABITUAL TENDENCIES ON THE ORGANISM

With each habitual tendency our organism too gets accordingly stirred up. The reason for this being so is easy to understand.

The various organs which constitute our organism, are but organs for the satisfaction of our will or thirst : the eyes for satisfying the will to see, the stomach for satisfying the will to digest and so forth. Accordingly, the organism as a whole is the very organ for satisfying will in general. Whenever we allow our organism to be in the service of any restless will stirring within us, this very restlessness will at the same time grasp at the organism itself, just as a rider feels any prance of his horse. Now any habitual tendency is, as we have seen, merely a symptom of our serving a desire with any of our organs of cognition. Such, however, is the interdependence of the organs of our organism, that any stirring up of our will in a particular sense organ affects the organism as a whole, with the same intensity with which it manifests itself in the respective habitual tendencies. This is the reason for the eyes to brighten when our will is being satisfied and accordingly the habitual tendency of joy arises in us, while they become dull and languid when our will is impeded, thus the habitual tendency of sadness being called forth. It is for the same reason that our body shakes and quivers when our will falls into the condition we call fright, and that our heart, as the central organ for satisfying our will to live, cramps with spasms when we suddenly face a peril of our life, our will to live being thereby shaken with utmost violence.

Thence important insights concerning the conservation of our health ensue: the more passionate (App. d.) the will stirring up in us, the more the organs concerned with its satisfaction are affected and therewith worn out, just as a steam-engine is shaken and worn out according to the power of the energy it generates. Now the most delicate organs for the content of will are the *nerves*; they specifically satisfy the will for *sensation*, thus being the sensory organs. For this reason they are affected more than other organs by craving, especially by a passionate one. Hence it follows that the best method to keep in healthy condition particularly one's nerves, and to recuperate those being strained, is not to allow one's will or craving to become too vehement, but to permanently *tranquillize* it; by doing so, we do calm our nerves too. A never failing way of achieving this tranquillity of will and therewith of our nerves is *serenity*: "Having achieved serenity, we become tranquil in body, tranquil in mind".

§ 21

THE POSSIBILITY OF THE DELIVERANCE OF THE MIND

We can now take up the question of whether we

can *free* ourselves from any will. This, however, presupposes this will or craving not to be a manifestation of our true Self, but a non-essential quality which merely arises in us and which we therefore can annihilate without being touched ourselves by doing so. In fact, this prooves to be true : A desire for something only arises in us as the result of our having recognized it as worthy of being possessed. It is inconceivable that we should desire to possess what we have recognised to be pain-producing. Now we have already seen that in reality nothing in the world is worth our taking the trouble, the whole world therewith being inadequate to us. Thence it follows that if we nevertheless crave for the world, this must be due to our *cognition* of the world being a false one; we do not see things in accordance with reality. Consequently, any craving or will for them is the result of a false cognition or of *ignorance* of their real nature. Let us assume a being finding himself suddenly and for the very first time in, let us say, a most vivid and exuberant scenery, with wholly developed sense-organs and in particular with a fully matured cognizing-faculty, still being *absolutely desireless*, without any will. He would look at the world like a boy who finds himself placed in an enchanted palace. As the boy would be marvelled at the beauty of the palace without seeing through the illusion, that being would take the world just *as it presents itself at the first glance*, that is, as extraordinarily beautiful and therewith as worthy of being desired. As a consequence thirst, *craving* for the world would arise in him, thus his fate being determined: his craving would increase with every day and soon become overwhelming; in all his activities he would be in its service. Consequently, on the break-down of his present organism with the inevitable death, that being would attach to a new germ for building up a new organism, at the end of which he would again grasp at a germ and so forth: as a result of this craving he would put himself into the world's hands for incalculable times, just as *we* have put ourselves in its hands too. Thus *our* craving too arises again and again: in the light of our consciousness or cognition (lit by our cognizing-apparatus) we regard the world as beautiful, so beautiful, that we grow unable to think of our true Self being beyond the world and that we therefore are left neither to the resources of this world nor to those of our organism or cognizing-apparatus.

This constant arising of new craving, as well as the strengthening of the thirst already in existence, takes place from time immemorial, since the very beginning of our entering the world cannot be made out; what is more, it is not even thinkable, just as the beginning of the world itself in its totality isn't: any chain of causality *necessarily* is beginningless, for it can consist of nothing but *alterations* — each alteration itself presupposing another one having preceded it, so that there cannot be a first one at all. However, a chain of causality is not necessarily *endless*; therefore, the chain of our rebirths isn't endless either!

§ 22

THE ANNIHILATION OF THIRST BY RIGHT COGNITION

Our *false cognition* of the world, i.e. our *ignorance* of its true, pain-producing and therewith inadequate nature, prevails from time immemorial. It results from a *wrong usage* of our cognizing-apparatus, be it through our regarding the world only superficially, i.e. taking into account but the present (App. e.) or by placing our cognizing-apparatus directly *in the service* of a prevailing *thirst*, thus making use of it with the sole purpose of finding out how best to satisfy it. Such being our practice since we are in the world, there has arisen within us an overwhelming thirst for further using our cognizing-apparatus in the selfsame way; finally not only our thirst for the world itself but for false cognition (in particular for false thinking) hinders us in the correct use of our cognizing-apparatus and, above all, from thinking correctly by its means.

Now this correct usage of our cognizing-apparatus consists in focusing it (without giving way to any influence or thirst) on the objects entering the field of our cognition; by doing so they not only present themselves as they are at present, but also in their future dissolution and therewith in their vanishing. The more we come to regard all objects in this way, therewith penetrating them in their actual relation to us (namely as *impermanent* phenomena), the more we shall realize them as being sorrow-bringing; accordingly, any thirst for them will be annihilated.

In other words : whatever we *wholly* recognize as impossible we cannot crave for; he who knows a lottery-ticket to be invalid, cannot feel the desire to win the first prize with it. Now once we have recognized *everything* in the world to be impermanent and at the same time achieve to make this cognition a constant one, we cannot crave or thirst for possessing anything forever. Therefore, he who despite all conceals such a thirst within him and thus laments and wails over the loss of the beloved object (i.e. over his will being impeded) is a fool. The wise man reckons in the loss of any object; therewith he constantly suppresses any desire to possess it for longer than the laws of nature allow. For this reason he doesn't mourn when the loss of the object becomes a fact; on the very contrary, he calms himself by clearly recognizing : "How could it be possible, that what has arisen and is doomed to destruction by its very nature, should not break down ? That is impossible".

§ 23

IN PARTICULAR THE DESIRE TO SEE OR COMMUNICATE WITH DEPARTED FRIENDS

Thus the correct usage of our cognizing-apparatus makes us consider the desire to possess something for longer than possible as the height of folly. Moreover, it brings about an additional insight, which is equally important and which we do already know: When a beloved being is snatched away from us by death, we know that what death has dissolved are but the "attributes" of the being, that he himself has not been touched at all by it. He merely has grasped at *new* attributes, for sensing and perceiving the world with this his new cognizing-apparatus; and he will do so eternally, as long as he *wants* to.

If he was a noble-minded being, he necessarily will attach to a noble world, according to the nobility of his willing; also if at his death he was better than at his birth he will attach to a world better than the one he left. Now why, if we really love a being, should we mourn over his now prosecuting his world-wandering as a happier being, under more favourable circumstances ? A motivation for mourning could be at most given when the departed being was evil, i.e. when he nourished a craving for the mean and harm-producing at the moment of his death and thus an unfortunate rebirth must be reckoned with. However, he would reap but what he has sown; later on, once the fruit of his evil action will be exhausted, he will again have the possibility of a moral ascent. *This* outlook is there for all beings, even for the most evil ones.

Certainly, in spite of all there still could be the desire to be united with the departed in his new form and world. This desire, however, may be brought to disappear by the following considerations: the departed has lost *any* remembrance of his last life and hence of me too, wherefore he doesn't at all miss me. From *his* point of view, there is nothing to be deplored, though from my point of view there is, for I do miss him. Now therewith I should admit to be mourning for my own sake. Moreover, even if my desire to be united with him should come true, he wouldn t recognize me due to his having assumed quite different attributes: may be the one or the other person which I now go past most indifferently on the street, has been my father, my mother or my child, my brother or my sister, in one of my countless former existences.

It is, of course, no rare occurrence, that the love to the deceased is strong enough to defy all such considerations. In this case the realization of the hope for reunion may, according to the Buddha, be counted upon. Thirst is, if only strong enough, almighty. At the moment of my death it will make me find out in the infinite universe the beloved being which had died before me; moreover, my thirst will infallibly bring about my attachment within the beloved being's range. Thus we shall meet again, though both in a new shape; although we shall not recognize one another, this reunion will deeply move both of us, calling forth a "love at first sight". All this may repeat several successive existences. Naturally, in the course of time, even in such a case estrangement shall gradually set in, wherewith even this love outlasting death shall prove to be *impermanent* (App. f.)

§ 24

THE ANNIHILATION OF CRAVING FOR THE OWN ORGANISM

Through the correct usage of our cognizing-apparatus we attain to *knowledge*. This knowledge is the insight, that "to crave for anything in the world" and "to crave for the impermanent and therewith for the sorrow-bringing" is all one, and that whatever we might lose and *must* lose according to the universal law never concerns the essence but only the outer form. This knowledge necessarily must bring about not only the vanishing of any thirst for these transient phenomena, but also of the thirst for prolonging the life of the cognizing-apparatus itself as the apparatus for perceiving this sorrow-bringing world. Moreover, any thirst for a new cognizing-apparatus at the dissolution of the present one at death, would equally die out, for it too would call forth but painful sensations in us, even though it were a cognizing-apparatus in the highest worlds of light: with all the pleasant sensations of the higher worlds, we must quit those worlds too, from what in the course of time necessarily ensues a gradual descent to the human or lower worlds, may be for countless thousands of years.

Is it possible for there to be any thinking man to deny that in him who *really* comprehends the whole of this survey of our abodes in the world (Cf. § 15) *any* thirst must become extinct?

§ 25

THE TRAINING OF THE THINKING-FACULTY THROUGH ITS METHODICAL DEVELOPMENT, AS PREREQUISITE FOR RIGHT COGNITION

The correct usage of our cognizing-apparatus is very difficult indeed. Nevertheless, the main point is that it *can* be achieved. The difficulty in using it in the aforesaid manner may be overcome by *practice*: in the course of time we shall succeed in performing any task, even though we were not accustomed to it, if only we practise. Practice is almighty. Master Eckhart, the great German mystic, says: "It is a question among people if it is possible to sin no more in this body. The best masters say that it is. This you must understand thus: these people have by inner and outer practice, come to inclining no more unto evil."

The proper way of regarding things is the following: *everything*, even our organism with its sensations and perceptions, is transient, therewith sorrow-bringing and consequently inadequate to us. Now in the beginning, the attempt to meditate in this manner upon things in a secluded place, appears to be almost impossible; we are constantly being disturbed by quite alien thoughts stirring up in us, like bubbles in stale water; we feel *compelled* to occupy ourselves with them, so that we deviate from the planned course before we are aware of it. This state of the mind is called *distraction*: one cannot concentrate exclusively upon *one* object. Distraction is the more difficult to overcome as those disturbing thoughts appear to be of *importance*, thus again tempting us to occupy ourselves with them. However, the question is to repeat the attempt not to yield to their seeming importance, but to continue meditating undisturbed in the purposed manner; we know only one thing to be of importance now: to get our thoughts under control. Thus we shall certainly come to realize "a gradual result": the disturbing thoughts lessen, the cognizing-activity becomes *purer* (purified from disturbing thoughts) and therewith *freer* and more independent, until in the course of time we shall manage to remain for hours deeply absorbed in peaceful contemplation.

This may also be achieved through a particular *training* : one endeavours e.g. to become wholly absorbed in the contemplation of a tree; then one tries to contemplate in the same manner a meadow; then, gradually increasing the area, a vast plain. Thus one can succeed in imagining *intuitively* an area of, let us say, Germany, in its full extension, as an immense, empty plane, free from any hills, forests, villages, towns etc. In fact, it *is* possible to survey with the mental eye *intuitively* a surface of such an extent ! This is, however, but one side of mental development, namely the aspect of extension. Running parallel to it there is the aspect of intensity. The following considerations may make it clear : there are dreams whose events are of such distinctness and clearness, that their vividness surpasses by far that of day-dreaming. Such dreams are the product of concentrated intuitive thinking, as a result of the calming down of any influences that could disturb the activity of the mind, the full energy of intuitive thinking thus being possible. This is why there often is hardly a difference between the clearness of such dreams and that of reality as it presents itself in day-consciousness. The purpose of thinking is the *repetition* of reality, the creation of a picture taken from the original. In *perfect* thinking repetition and reality, picture and original, wholly coincide and are equally clear. Now just this highest degree of intuitive thinking is the other side of the aforesaid mental development, i.e. that concerning the intensity of the concentration on *one* object of contemplation. To him who in secluded contemplation attains to this degree of concentration of the mind, his corporeal organism presents itself with *utter clearness* as a product of seized materials of the external nature, and therewith as absolutely non-essential; moreover, all phenomena, including this organism itself, present themselves with the same evident clearness as transient and therewith sorrow-bringing. How poor, how terribly weak appears to be on the other hand *our* much praised development of mental faculties, and how far away are to be marked out the bounds of the impossible! How overwhelming must therefore be the conclusions such highly developed thinking-faculty must come to! Who would ever doubt that he who has methodically developed his power of thinking in this way, will bring to an end the eternal fight between light and darkness with the triumph of light? This fight has much been pictured since olden times. It simply depicts the battle of pure contemplation against ignorance, the latter manifesting itself uninterruptedly in wrong thinking; this very ignorance is the cause of our suffering from the *delusion* of belonging to the world and of it being a pleasure to live in it.

§ 26

THE GRADUAL OVERCOMING OF THIRST

The more we sharpen the weapon of right cognition, the more it shall serve us to fight against our *thirst*, thus fighting the very battle in which our life-work actually consists. It is the fight which the religions symbolize as the battle with the Evil One, with the dragon, or otherwise.

In this fight, every inch of territory must be wrested from the enemy through intense training: First of all, we must become *upright* men, i.e. such men as do not yield to the *gross* manifestations of thirst; to surrender to them means to satisfy one's thirst at the expense of the other beings, thus falling below the bounds of the human world. He who doesn't observe those limits, runs the risk of being reborn in the sub-human realms.

The first step upon the path of virtue is to endeavour to achieve moral purity. It consists in upright conduct having become a *trait of our character*; this we attain to when we need not fight our thirst again and again, that is, when those manifestations of our thirst which are contrary to moral purity have been definitively extinguished. At this stage we may expect to be reborn in the human world or in lower heavenly spheres.

Having thus attained the first stage, we may aim at disinteresting ourselves in any *worldly* things as next goal of our moral striving, i.e. try to wholly suffocate our thirst in this regard. Naturally, this detachment needs not necessarily manifest itself in outer poverty; it is rather a question of an *inner* one: one doesn't cling any longer to what one owns. Consequently, one doesn't make use of it in one's own interest but exclusively in that of the fellow-beings: "He who though adorned fosters a serene mind, is calm, controlled, pure and has ceased to injure other beings: he is a brāhmin, an ascetic, a monk" (*Dha.* v. 142). The immediate result of this annihilation of the thirst for worldly pleasure is, apart from the absolute equanimity as concerns everything in the world, our giving way to unlimited *altruism*; this is the reason why at this stage one is bound up in an active friendliness towards all beings. This degree of moral perfection may bring about rebirth in the Brahma-world, or in the Christian heaven in its purest form: the inhabitants of these spheres have lost any interest in worldly property and worldly pleasure, thus being poor in the common sense of the word. Moreover, those realms are such of purest love and absolute friendliness (mettā). The Buddha declares that those men who, while still on earth, live in voluntary detachment and in total purity (together with unlimited friendliness towards all living creatures), do live "a heavenly life on earth" (quasi coelestem vitam in terris ab omni caducarum rerum cura et cupiditate alienam). "Brahma I know, and the world of Brahma I know, and the path leading to the world of Brahma I know .... There the disciple penetrates with benevolent mind one cardinal point, and so he penetrates the second and the third and the fourth. He penetrates and fills upward and downwards and horizontally the whole world, everywhere, completely, with benevolent mind, deep, great, all-embracing, beyond all measure, free from enmity, free from ill-will." Then the same is said of a compassionate mind, and of a mind filled with sympathetic joy and equanimity. (*Digha-Nik.*, 13. Sutta).

Therewith we have reached the perfection of morality and the ultimate goal of all religions. They declare; "We do not grasp anything higher than this." Thus from this very point begins the absolute lack of comprehension of the great majority of men with regard to the kernel of the doctrine of the Buddha. The Buddha's disciple may attain while yet alive states higher than the state of Brahma-heaven: through pure cognizing-activity culminating in deep contemplation, he suffocates also *any* thirst for whatever perceptions of multiplicity; thus, wholly deaf and blind to the external world, he may enjoy for hours or even days the only and exclusive perception of *infinite space*. To get at least an idea of the magnitude of this deliverance of the mind, one has but to consider that *we* hardly achieve concentrating our mind on one object only even for a few seconds without being disturbed by our thirst, while the aforesaid disciple of the Buddha remains for days, absolutely undisturbed, in the contemplation of the infinite void space. After his death, he will be reborn beyond the Brahma-world, in a sphere adequate to him: a sphere in which he enjoys the majestic solitude and the supra-mundane peace of void space, thus not facing death for millions of years.

But even this is not the pinnacle. Even the thirst for this and similar forms of existence can be overcome. This is achieved by regarding them too as being impermanent and hence sorrow-bringing, until there remains nothing but "this body equipped with the six senses, as condition of life", that is, it is left the mere *apparatus* for cognizing, without *any* craving for further making use of it: everything, in the widest sense of the word, has been realized as transitory, sorrow-bringing and hence inadequate to us, so that no thirst at all can stir within us. "Mind, now thoroughly peaceful, may contemplate the annihilation of thirst" — "Done is, what was to be done" (*Majjh.-Nik.*, 7. Sutta). When I have no more will for having recognized *everything* what I could have ever wanted to possess, according to reality as sorrow-bringing, and when I thus have no further use in particular for my cognizing-activity (having already recognized whatever is cognizable), what else could I desire but to become extinct? (With regard to the concept of "extinction", see § 30). "A peaceful one I am, an extinguished one I am, a no longer grasping one" (*Majjh.-Nik.*, 102. Sutta). Such a man has wholly realized the *deliverance of his mind,* he is not "led by the dreadful craving" any longer, he has attained "the highest, the holy freedom" : he is now absolutely free in the use of his cognizing-apparatus, without being influenced by any thirst; he is absolutely detached from it. Thus he has fought to the victorious end the very fight against the mighty opponent, the *thirst* for the world. He has become a Delivered One. (App. g.)

§ 27

THE DELIVERANCE OF THE MIND IS THE FREEDOM IN THE USE OF OUR COGNIZING-APPARATUS

The problem of mental deliverance, i.e. of absolute deliverance and non-disturbance in the use of our cognizing-apparatus, regarded from the highest point of view, presents itself as follows: everything in the world is, at bottom, sorrow-bringing for us. Accordingly, the best thing to do would be not to make any further use of our cognizing-apparatus. Strange to say, however, we are not in a position to do so without more ado. Thus the problem of the freedom of our mind is, at bottom, the problem of how it comes that we aren't able *not* to make use of our cognizing-apparatus whenever we want. The Buddha's answer is that we are being continually *compelled*, often with a force which seems to be irresistible, to use it; in other words : he shows us that will, whose satisfaction is the sole purpose of our making use of our cognizing-apparatus, has the nature of *craving*. As soon as this craving has been annihilated, I may just as well use my cognizing-apparatus or use it not : what could then ever hinder me particularly from not using it any more ? Now this craving can, of course, only be annihilated through the correct use of our cognizing-apparatus and through the cognition ensuing therefrom, namely the cognition of any craving or will being silly, yea wrong, since it can be aimed but at what is sorrow-bringing.

Certainly we are also restricted in this cognizing-activity itself; first because of its quality (it may be rather poor), and then owing to the circumstances we must live in often impeding a right cognizing-activity. However, all these are but *external* hindrances and, at bottom, due to craving themselves. Because of this, precisely this our craving brought about our attachment to a germ of the kind and in the circumstances from which our actual organism as well as its environment ensued. By ennobling our thirst we may thus effect the condition for clinging to a better germ in more appropriate circumstances on our coming death; thus our next cognizing-apparatus, and the circumstances we shall then live in, will be more favourable for a proper cognizing-activity. Now this *ennobling* of our thirst we can in any case bring about just now.

Hence it follows, that the annihilation of thirst takes place gradually: the animal is being wholly determined by its craving or instincts (which are but the manifestations of thirst in particular) in the use of its cognizing-apparatus. Because of this its mind is wholly *undelivered.* Not much, but a little bit better do things go with the majority of men. They take it for a matter of course that one can do, and does, only what one feels a desire for; therefore almost the whole of their activity, and in particular the cognizing one, is in the service of their *thirst.* But even in the morally lowest man, who has sold his deliverance to the thirst at the price of mean sense-pleasures, a trace of pure activity is left, i.e. of an activity not influenced by any thirst. Now this very trace of freedom in the usage of one's cognizing-apparatus may, if only applied to the achievement of right cognition, serve as a basis for gradually checking thirst, thus increasing the deliverance more and more in the course of time. For this reason *every* man has the possibility of dying better than he was born. Thus causing his thirst to decrease from existence to existence (what manifests itself in the thirst becoming *nobler*), he may in time attain to the absolute *annihilation* of thirst.

We ourselves, living in a "Black Age", normally must content with such a gradual progress extending itself over existences; yet we have no right to complain of it. for we haven't deserved anything better in our former lives. Naturally, this development progresses more quickly with the one than with the other.

This freedom of the cognizing-activity through fighting the thirst the *upright* man strives for to a considerable degree, while the *morally pure* one considerably realizes it. He who has annihilated any thirst for *worldly* objects, has attained a high degree of deliverance; therewith he has become overripe for this earth and will thus emigrate to the Brahma-world. In this way, the deliverance increases more and more, until finally, with the annihilation of *any* thirst, it becomes an absolute one: all compulsion to mental activity has come to its end; one can stop without difficulty any such activity, i.e. all seeing, hearing, smelling, tasting, touching and thinking. Therewith one will have become a *really* great man: "'A great man, a great man it is said, Lord; but in what respect is one a great man ?'—'If one has delivered (i.e. freed from any influence of any thirst) the mind (i.e. the whole of the mental activities), Sāriputta, then one is a great man; if one surrenders the mind (to thirst), one is not'" (*Samy.-Nik.*, XLVII, 11).

§ 28

THE BLISS OF NON-WILLING

Hitherto we repeatedly touched on the bliss of the deliverance of the mind. The main point now, however, is to become quite clear on the following: we desire happiness, and nothing else. To sum up, life may be characterized as a pursuit of happiness. What is more: we desire the utmost happiness, which ends in bliss.

Now what is happiness? To begin with, it is but the dissolution of a tormenting *thirst* or craving through its satisfaction. We consider the attainment of any possession or goal as happiness only when we had *striven* for them formerly, i.e. when we have had a craving for them. This happiness will be the greater, the stronger the craving now stilled had been whereas it will be absolute when the craving has been annihilated *forever.* Now we use to live for the most part only in the present and for the present; thus we do not recognize the *true* happiness of the *permanent* deliverance from a painful thirst: he who suffers chronically from a serious illness, regards even the slightest temporary betterment (i.e. every temporary satisfaction of his thirst for restoration of his health) as great happiness. As the greatest happiness, however, he regards the moment of his complete recovery. Then he will feel glad, lucky, extremely happy, for now his craving is wholly satisfied. But this his happiness will decrease in the same degree in which the recovery persists; finally it will cease entirely, although it is in this *persistence* that perfect bodily well-being lies.

All this confirms two facts: the greatest happiness with regard to the organism is that in which no thirst concerning it stirs; furthermore, that true happiness is not merely a momentary emotion, but a *constant, absolute well-being,* which as such needs not necessarily become an object of consciousness. Now as with the happiness concerning the organism, so with the true happiness on the whole; the less *thirst* or will an individual has, the better off he is, and having no thirst whatever he reaches the highest, perfect well-being and therewith the highest bliss. This he attains to in spite of, i.e. because of his not knowing rapturous emotions any longer; (the latter are not the manifestation of the invariable, perfect well-being, but merely of momentary, transient everyday happiness). Thus he has attained the "perfect contentment, the highest tranquility", and consequently the "truly desirable state." Thus it is a matter of fact that true happiness increases in the same degree in which one advances in virtue by first controlling one's thirst, then by ennobling and finally by wholly suffocating it. Thus it comes that serenity is a characteristic trait not only of moral men, but in particular of the inhabitants of the higher realms. "We do live happily, we who possess nothing. Living on joy, we are like the pure gods" (*Dhp*. v. 200).

How immense must then be the absolute well-being of him who is wholly delivered from thirst, who wants absolutely nothing, to whom *anything* is superfluous: "Of what use is a well to one who has water?" — "Who so has uprooted craving, what should he strive for any more?" asks the Master. It is the happiness which Schopenhauer suggests when he says: "That we feel so unspeakably happy if set free for a moment from the grim urgency of willing, leaves us to conjecture how blissful must be the life of a man whose will is wholly stilled; freed from the torments of desire and fear he observes smilingly the illusory phantasms of this world which had beset and tormented him, like chessmen scattered about the board after the game is ended. If we picture to ourselves the heavenly peace of such a life we shall hunger for it from the depths of our own misery and despair, since willing (in the guise of greed, fear, envy, anger) binds us fast, pulling us hither and thither with a thousand cords." (*World as Will and Representation*, Vol. I, Chap. 68.) Thus the only adequate condition for us is that in which any craving, any will is forever extinguished. Just consider: a man who has *no* further will, who has caused this "deepest, darkest, most mysterious force of nature" to disappear, who thus no longer is compelled to use his cognizing-apparatus for satisfying any thirst or desire! Could there be anything more sublime, more peaceful than this absolute will-lessness? (App. h.) Is not this state the truly divine one, all the more as it is, in contrast to that of the inhabitants even of the highest heavens, *unchangeable*, beyond space and time? It cannot be disturbed any more by anything, not even by the vanishing of the own organism and therewith of the whole world. On the very contrary: with the definitive cast-off of the organism as the apparatus of suffering and thereby with the definitive withdrawal from the world of sorrow, the perfect well-being becomes the *absolute* bliss, the very possibility of further disturbance thus being forever removed. (App. i.) There is hardly any other meditation for accomplishing the destruction of thirst, like that on "the bliss of deliverance consisting in the annihilation of craving."

THE EXTINGUISHED SELF

§ 29

THE SELF IS TRANSCENDENT: *ALL* CONCEPTS APPLY ONLY TO THE *NOT-SELF* (ANATTĀ)

"Whatever lies within the domain of concepts, the domain of definitions, the domain of cognition, that is the corporeal organism together with consciousness" (*Dīgha-Nik.*, XV); in their interdependence both of them result in the *personality.* These our "attributes" are the object of any possible cognition. According to them, we are determined and differentiated from each other as Mr. X and Mrs. Y. The Accomplished One definitely discards these "attributes" (i.e. his personality) at his death. Thus, from this moment on, he has become undeterminable, yea wholly uncognizable: "That *by what he had been defined* no longer exists". How could *he* be defined who has no more organism, who therewith doesn't any longer sense and perceive, who no longer thinks, who no longer *desires* anything at all?

Since all concepts concerning us apply only to our "attributes", from which alone they are derived, they do not apply to our true Self. Thus it is a fact that in him who recognizes whatever he carries with him, according to reality as mere "attributes", not even the mere *thought* on his Self may arise. It is, however, quite different with *us*: we do identify ourselves with our "attributes." Consequently, out of ignorance, we do not distinguish our true Self from what we *erroneously* take for our essence. As a result, we apply the laws to which our pseudo-self (also called the empirical self or the personality) is subject to our true Self. For this reason the ultimate truth must appear to us as full of contradictions, wholly in agreement with Schopenhauer, who says that whenever we find contradictions in the world, it is because we take to be one what is two. How can *I*, for instance, be reborn, if *I* have died, i.e. if *I* have been dissolved? Isn't this an obvious contradiction, since what does not exist any longer cannot be reborn? Strange to say, some people do torment themselves with this seeming contradiction, putting forward the most abstruse hypotheses to eliminate it. Yet in reality there exists no such contradiction. I just must not "take for one what is two", I must but realize that the concepts of dying and of being reborn define processes which apply but to my "attributes" and not to my true Self. Thus it is easy to understand, that *I myself* may experience many innumerable times the sensation of dying (in the dissolution of my "attributes") and of being reborn (in the building-up of my new "attributes"), just as one may again and again take off one dress and put on another one, experiencing on each occasion the respective sensations.

§ 30

THE CONCEPT OF EXTINCTION IN PARTICULAR

What most has given (and still gives) rise to misunderstandings, is the fact that the Buddha calls an Accomplished One after death a "totally extinguished one" (parinibbuto). Now some scholars consider the concept "totally extinguished" to be far beyond any doubt and wholly clear : they declare it to state the absolute annihilation of the object it concerns, so that it seems there not to be any other way to interpret it. Therefrom again ensues a contradiction, and what is more, a very serious one, namely with the fact that the Accomplished One is not at all touched by his death: on the very contrary, his death causes his perfect well-being to become an absolute one. However, those scholars did not succeed in removing that contradiction; they accept the two apparently diametrically opposed statements only as an alternative, declaring the Buddha to have taught *either* the absolute extinction of the saint with his death, *or* his being in no way touched by it. It is characteristic of our modern, altogether materialistic age with its hate for the transcendent, that there are also interpretations which have decided on the first alternative, i.e. that of absolute extinction *in the sense of absolute annihilation.* And that despite the Buddha's repeated assurances that he does *not* teach annihilation but, on the contrary, the path to the "*Imperishable*", namely imperishable in the sense of "beyond space and time." Let us refer to one among many examples: at Eka-Nipāta of the *Aṅguttara Nikāya* XXI, the "*Imperishable*" is solemnly proclaimed not less than *twenty-four times* as highest goal. Could the Buddha ever have expressed it clearer ?

In reality both the concept of absolute extinction and of not being touched by death do not at all contradict each other. They rather combine to yield a harmonious whole. In fact, the Accomplished

One is extinguished at death just as a *lamp* is extinguished; actually the Buddha himself uses this simile. Now the lamp itself is not at all touched either by its burning or by its becoming extinct. Both the burning and the extinction are mere processes which concern but the "attributes" of the lamp, namely oil and wick. In just the same way life and extinction of life are mere processes which do not touch in the slightest degree my true Self. This my true Self is beyond *life*; now life is the sum of any sensations (to live = to sense), and nothing else but these sensations and the thirst which calls them forth becomes extinguished by death. This is why my true Self cannot be touched by their extinction. If in spite of this it is said that the Accomplished One himself is extinguished, it is due to the very same linguistic usage by which we say that the lamp itself becomes extinct.

The state of affairs is the same when *fire* itself is said to extinguish. This is why the Buddha brings into play the extinction of *fire* to illustrate the extinction of an Accomplished One: the fire too consists as little in the fuel and in the flame it brings about, as man in his personality. If only the fire could cognize, it too would declare of the flame and the fuel (and of the greed with which it grasps the fuel to produce the flame), what the Delivered One declares of his personality: "This is not mine, this I am not, this is not my true Self". That what underlies the manifestation of fire is therefore also an Unfathomable (-X-), in which arises *thirst*, consequently the *grasping* of fuel taking place. Thus the *becoming* of a process of combustion goes on. (App. j.)

According to this combustion or to the shining-element it calls forth, the X underlying the whole process is itself called fire; in the very same way we too are defined by our "attributes" and cannot be defined otherwise.

This deep clarification of the process of combustion was already known to the authors of the Upanishads, as we find, for instance, in passages as the following: "Like fire, *when the wood is burnt up*" — "Just as the fire is at rest in its realm when the fire-wood is consumed" — "Brahman is in his nature pure thinking, like the fire which has consumed the fire-wood". (App. k. and l.) — "As the fire, when it entered its homestead, persists invisibly in its own nature..." (Deussen, 60 *Upanishads*). "Just as of the fire that flames up under the strokes of the smith's hammer it cannot be said where it has gone after it is extinguished, so just as little can be discovered the abode of the truly Delivered Ones who have crossed over the stream of the bonds of the senses, have reached the unshakable bliss" (*Udāna* VIII, 10). How superficial and limited but to the external process appear in comparison with this our scientific theories on the process of combustion!

Moreover, the Buddha *expressly* teaches that what becomes extinct of ours are but the flames of greed, of hatred and of delusion, i.e. the three manifestations of *thirst*. For this reason he defines the extinction (nibbāna) also as thirst-extinction (tanhā-nibbāna), or as the *extinction of will*: "The holy life under the Sublime One is lived for the extinction of craving" (*Samy.-Nik.*, LI, 15).

§ 31

THE CONCEPT OF NOTHINGNESS

To cognize means: "there are objects for me." Accordingly, to discard the cognizing-apparatus means: "there are no (sorrow-bringing) objects for me and therewith there is no-thing at all." Thus the very concept of "nothing" applies only and exclusively to the domain of the *not-Self* and denotes merely the absence of the domain of the not-Self (the world) for me. The concept of "nothing" presupposes *me* who think it; therefore the antithesis of the world is not absolute nothingness but my true Self. Consequently, there is in reality but a relative nothingness, i.e. a nothingness but for cognition, hence a nothingness only in the sense of "nothing of that which we cognize" and never an absolute nothingness which would include my own annihilation. What is more, such an absolute nothingness, if closely considered, is not even thinkable and hence absolutely impossible. This ensues from the following:

I myself am beyond the impermanent, i.e. beyond space and time. This is not a mere *belief* in a transcendent Self as some people think it is, but the surest fact to exist. This absolute certainty is gained through the intuitive insight that all the transient and therewith space- and time-bound components of my personality cannot be my true Self and that I in my deepest essence am in no way touched by their dissolution: what we perceive originating and perishing, cannot be assumed to be our true Self. This must become quite clear to us, in order that we may be able, despite its extraordinary simplicity, to penetrate it in all its depth and inner obviousness. Note especially that the Buddha does not say: what originates and perishes, is not my Self. *This* sentence might be disputed, as it might not be clear at once why something transient might not constitute my true Self. The Buddha says: "What I *perceive* originating and perishing, that cannot be my true Self"; this statement will certainly not be doubted by any thinking creature. For what I *perceive* to originate and to perish must with logical consequence be something different from me. For if I were identical with the disappearing object, along with its disappearing I also should have ceased to exist. But I am still there after the object is gone. Therefore it was not my self nor anything belonging to *me*. (Cf. *The Doctrine of the Buddha*, p. 115). He who in spite of all maintains to be able to think the thought of absolute nothingness, certainly has a false concept of himself as the thinking subject: he falsely considers himself to consist in the impermanent components of his personality. By doing so there is, of course, room for an absolute nothingness after the dissolution of those components. Now where there is no thinking, there is no nothingness either, for this is always but a *thought*. He who deems that he thinks away himself on thinking absolute nothingness, actually considers as absent or non-existent but what he had *improperly* put into the concept of Self. It is just like declaring that one was able to think the concept of wooden iron. Consequently, to him who cognizes according to reality, even the mere thought of an absolute nothingness (and therewith of his own annihilation) is impossible. (App. m.)

§ 32

THE ABSOLUTE STATE

"If we practise introspection thoroughly, we shall find that we are not in an absolute state and that time is not essential to us, a fact which has been expressed long before Kant by philosophers and mystics; and we shall find that also the possession of a cognizing-apparatus, and thus the faculty to cognize itself are alike non-essential. We even perceive a longing for freedom from all those determinants (what seems to me to be the foundation of all true philosophical aspirations). Thus it must be a state in which no cognizing-activity takes place, in which therefore there is no object, nor am I, accordingly, subject; therewith, in that state there is nothing analogous to my consciousness either, and though in the latter there is a striving and an anticipation of it, no definition of it can, however, be made, because of its being beyond any reason." (Words by Schopenhauer in Buddhist version; *Frauenstaedt*, *Schopenhauers handschr. Nachlass*, p. 219.)

§ 33

THE "SUBMERGING IN ONE'S OWN DEPTHS"
OR
THE IMMEASURABILITY OF THE ABSOLUTE STATE

To be without any desire for forms, for sounds, for scents, flavours, tactile objects and thoughts;

therewith without desire for sensation and perception, which are but the sensation and perception of those forms, sounds, scents, flavours, tactile objects and thoughts;

thus to be without desire for consciousness or cognition, which consist but in this sensation and perception;

hence without desire for a corporeal organism as the *apparatus* for the production of sensations and perceptions and therewith for becoming conscious or for cognizing;

in short: to be *absolutely desireless, will-less*.

This absolute will-lessness "does not at all mean the annihilation of a substance, but the mere act of non-willing. That which willed hitherto wills no longer. Since we know this essence—(our true Self)—only in and by the act of willing, we, the subjects of cognition, are not in a position to say or to grasp what it furthermore is or does when it has given up this act" (Schopenhauer, *Parerga II*). To our cognition that absolute will-lessness is therefore a transition to nothingness.

Properly considered, this uncognizable — (our true Self) —might be of such sublimity and majesty, that if one could grasp it, one should be altogether amazed at one's having fled *this* state instead of aspiring it as the highest. In fact, this our uncognizable essence *is* the most sublime and majestic : in it there is no arising and passing away. The world in all its temporal and spatial infinity is "only the measure of one's own grandeur, always surpassing it" (Schopenhauer). But by this, be it well noted, at bottom, nothing positive is affirmed, but only one's unlimitedness, hence something purely negative. From the standpoint of the saint, it is not he who disappears, but the world. To us the process presents itself as just the reverse. (Cf. *The Doctrine of the Buddha*, pp. 266-267.)

"What do you think, Mahārāja, have you got a calculator, a mint-master or a teller, who might be able to count the sands of the Ganges, who might be able to say : 'So many grains of sand, or so many hundreds or thousands of grains of sand are there ?' — 'That I have not, Reverend One'. — 'Or have you got a calculator, a mint-master or a teller who might be able to measure the water of the great Ocean, who might be able to say : 'So many quarts of water, or so many hundreds or thousands of quarts of water are contained therein ?' — 'That I have not, Reverend One' — 'And why not ?' — 'Because the great Ocean is deep, immeasurable, unfathomable.' — 'Even so it is, Mahārāja, if you wish to understand the essence of an Accomplished One according to the predicates of corporeality, of sensation, of perception, of the activities of the mind, of cognition (consciousness). In an Accomplished One this corporeality, this sensation, this perception, these activities of the mind, this cognition would be extinguished, uprooted, so that they would not be able to develop again. The Accomplished One, Mahārāja, is free from this, that his essence might be counted with numerals of the corporeal world: he is deep, immeasurable, unfathomable like the great Ocean'". (*Samy.* – *Nik.*, XLIV, 1). Only this may be said, that his state is "freedom from any motion", "profound silence", "great stillness", "the absolute tranquility" (App. n.); in short, the "Great Peace".

Thus we divine the Ineffable.

§ 34

THE REALM OF ESSENCES

Nothing in the world is a Being, but a mere Becoming (bhava). Yet any Becoming, as for instance that of fire too (cf. § 30), is, as we have already seen, conditioned by an *attachment* or *grasping*, which in itself is but realized *willing*. Now any will presupposes an essence which lies *behind* the will and therewith beyond the world of Becoming; it is an unfathomable X. Any cognition in accordance with reality ultimately amounts to this dualism. Yet this dualism is not an absolute one, for each phenomenon or "attribute" is *conditioned* by the will of the X which underlies it : were any willing to extinguish, any Becoming (and hence the whole world as the sum of all the different processes of Becoming) too would be abolished. Nevertheless, it wouldn't be touched there by the *realm of essences* or the *sphere beyond extinction* (Nibbānadhātu) : "Just as all waters of the earth and of the air do flow into the great Ocean, and yet the great Ocean neither increases nor decreases, even so does the sphere of Nibbāna, free from any "attributes", neither increase nor decrease, however many noble disciples might submerge in it" (*Udāna* V, 5). (App. o.)

This sphere of Nibbāna is the *home* of all the X on whose willing the countless *phenomena* called "world" depend; therefore it is said of the extinguished fire, as of the extinguished Accomplished One, that they have "gone home". With regard to the extinguished Accomplished Ones this home is in particular named "the abode of the vanished Awakened Ones, who have overcome the circle of rebirths".

Therewith the farthest bound of any possible cognition is reached. The relation of these X to one another is absolutely uncognizable, for they are transcendent, beyond any cognition. They are, however, so little a *unity,* that in their "attributes" (as world) they constantly tear one another to pieces; but they aren't a *plurality* either, wherefore they may unite in their "attributes" in all-embracing love. What remains is — silence. To declare the realm of essences to be the one primitive entity, or the Brahman, or the absolutum, or the thing-in-itself would be but a mere speculation about the uncognizable.

In any case, however, absolute harmony reigns in the sphere of Nibbāna, in the realm of the Absolute, for the beings submerged in it. Therefrom ensues as the moral principle in the phenomenal world: *unlimited benevolence.*

"Om Amitaya ! Measure not with words
th' Immeasurable, nor sink the plumb of thought
into the Fathomless ! Who asks doth err,
who answers, errs. Say naught !" (App. p.).

APPENDIX

a :

Even the heat produced by these chemical alterations partly derives from the external nature. It is, after all, the heat of the sun, chemically bound by grains etc. in the process of ripening, thus remaining *latently* in them. During the process of assimilation, this heat bound to the food again becomes free and penetrates the whole body as vital warmth. Thus, the very warmth of my body depends on the heat which, a few months ago, was many millions of miles from this earth, a fact which makes it obvious that even heat is not essential to *me*.

b :

The Buddha distinguishes three kinds of worlds: the world of sensual pleasure (to which our world belongs), the world of pure forms and the formless worlds. In the worlds of pure forms the beings still are clad with an organism, but any sensual craving, in particular any sexual desire and therewith any sexuality has been overcome by them. Therefore, in the *pure worlds* there are no sexually differentiated bodies. For this reason, nobody can reach those worlds who still has a craving for sexuality. They are the worlds of noble joy of contemplation — without craving for anything —, joys which, by way of exception, a noble man may experience while on earth (e.g. while contemplating a magnificent scenery or the starry sky); they are the worlds of aesthetic contemplation. In the *formless worlds* there is only a craving for the contemplation of the infinite space in its peaceful majesty and similar conditions.

c :

We accept the fact that we cannot remember the events of our early childhood as a matter of course; and we take it for granted that such a recollection would presuppose constant endeavour in training our memory, by trying gradually to recall more and more remote scenes, until finally the events of our earliest childhood dawn upon consciousness. We expect, nevertheless, in case the doctrine of reincarnation is true, to be able to recall our former existences *without more ado* and without any training of the mind. "Even with regard to this my present life, Lord, I am not able to recollect in details what I have experienced. How then should I recollect various former forms of existence?" (*Majjh.–Nik.*, 79. Sutta).

A more plausible objection lies in the problem of how such recollection is possible, in view of the fact that everything in us, and hence in particular consciousness, constantly arises anew, so that past events cannot at all be stored there. In fact, the organ of thought as well as the brain and the consciousness are absolutely out of the question as *receptacles* of any memories; thus there is not to be found something like microscopic plates of all our countless experiences in them. These rather sink into our unfathomable essence, which is not touched by any alteration, impressing themselves upon it. From there memories are raised to consciousness at any given time, in the way of the *association of ideas,* through our *will.*

d :

By passion we understand a chronic slavery of the cognizing-activity to a particular *craving,* i.e. a slavery which has become habitual by our serving this thirst for a series of successive lives. The consequence is that whenever that particular thirst arises, we are instantly subjected to extremely vehement habitual tendencies.

e :

The presence is but one instant, while the future is the infinite sum of all the presences following the actual one. Thus, if I concern myself for the future, I do so for countless presences. The everyday man concerns himself only for the *one* presence which has become real.

f :

Certain spiritualistic and theosophical circles cultivate the desire to communicate with the departed before the own death, i.e. during the present life. According to the Buddha, there is a prospect of fulfilment of this desire only with regard to those departed who are still earth-bound, i.e. who have passed away with a monoideism focused upon the circumstances under which they had lived in their former existence. Thus they re-objectify in the very realm which allows a communication with their former environments : in the *realm of shades.*

A communication with the departed reborn into higher realms is only possible when and as far as these higher realms have become reality in one's own mind while on earth.

g :

The difference between the relation of an Accomplished One and of an average man to their corporeal organism as the cognizing-apparatus, may be illustrated as follows : Finding myself in the dark and wanting to see a certain object, I strike a match and try to satisfy my curiosity during the life of the match. If I succeed in doing so, I look with indifference upon its coming extinction; if, however, the match nears its end and I have not yet sufficiently cognized the object in question, I shall try by every possible means to prolong its life, and when, finally, it does go out, I shall light another match in the endeavour to satisfy my desire for cognition. In this simile, the match stands for our cognizing-apparatus, with which we constantly endeavour to satisfy our thirst for cognition. As long as this thirst has not yet been completely satisfied, we must get stirred up at the menace of the break-down of this apparatus and try to save it by every possible means. And when, finally, it does die, we immediately look for and secure a new one. The saint, however, recognizes *everything* as sorrow-bringing; in particular he recognizes as sorrow-bringing his corporeal organism as mere *apparatus* for cognizing, i.e. for the sensation and perception of the sorrow-bringing. Therefore the saint watches the disintegration of this apparatus with absolute indifference, without even the vaguest desire to stir in him.

h :

"The former greed and will and selfishness he was filled with when he was an ignorant, are now got rid of by him, cut off at the root, made like a palm-tree-stump that can come to no future growth" (*Majjh.-Nik.*, 140. Sutta). Considering this state of a Perfected One, how could one declare man's will to be his true Self, the real kernel of his essence, as Schopenhauer does? If the saint would put himself the question : "What am I ?", he couldn't think of being *will* himself, just because he *has no more will.* The saint has lost his will completely and yet he is; he is all the more, namely an absolutely happy one, who has attained the highest bliss. Hence what he has lost was no part of his essence. At *Itivuttaka* 15 the Buddha calls tanhā, the craving thirst, the "dutiyā", i.e. the *companion.* In reality, "dutiyā" means "the second one" and is in particular used instead of "wife".

i :

This illustrates clearly that the Buddhist saint stands far above the Christian one. Certainly the Christian saint too has fulfilled his master's exhortation to overcome the world; in this case, however, the world overcome by both the master and the disciple is only *our* world of sensual craving, but not the world of pure forms and the formless worlds, which belong to the world as well. The Buddhist saint, on the contrary, has overcome the *whole* world and all its heavens. Even the Sotāpanno, having attained the lowest degree of Buddhist holiness, has "entered the Stream" leading to the overcoming of *all* forms of existence.

j :

Fire is not the chemical compound of fuel and oxygen, but this compound — due to the *grasping* of fuel and oxygen from the depths of the Unfathomable— calls forth a *new* element, namely fire, called the shining-element. Naturally this applies to *all* chemical compounds: if hydrogen and oxygen combine in a proportion of 2 : 1, a *new* element, liquid, which brings about water, is called forth from the Unfathomable. Thus water doesn't consist of H_2O but is merely the *prerequisite* for the liquid element (and therewith for water) to appear.

k :

Such passages make it clear that it used to be a matter of course to the Indians, that fire is not annihilated through its extinction, but that it merely returns home, for which reason they say that the fire has *gone home*. With regard to this the Buddha declares that a dead Delivered One has done just what the fire has: he became extinct, he went home; there is but one difference : in contrast to the fire, the Delivered One goes home *forever*.

l :

From the last passage it also follows to what extent the authors of the Upanishads do not come up to the Buddha : although they too do compare the Brahman (the Self) with the extinguished fire, they attribute *thinking* to it. The Buddha, however, has recognized even thinking as a non-essential function of ours, performed by means of the cognizing-apparatus and bound to it.

m :

From the preceding elucidations, the one or the other might gain a further insight : any ignorance, and therewith any mischief in the world, has its source in false thinking. From this unskill in thinking, which we do not manage to wholly get rid of with all our mental culture, it may be deduced how non-essential even this thinking (and thus any cognizing-activity) must be to us.

n :

Words by Master Eckhardt.

o :

The Canon distinguishes four spheres : kāma-dhātu, the sphere of sensual craving; rūpa-dhātu, the sphere of pure forms; arūpa-dhātu, the formless sphere, and nibbāna-dhātu, the sphere in which any thirst or craving is extinct (therefore also called tanhā-nibbāna). (Cf. App. b.)

p :

E. Arnold, *The Light of Asia.*